The Devil, the Angel, and the Referee

Understanding Freud's Id, Ego, and Superego

Freudian Trips

Contents

Copyright Page

Published by Omniterra Media Inc

First Edition

Visit the author's website at www.freudiantrips.com

Disclaimer

The views and opinions expressed in this book are those of the author(s) and do not necessarily reflect the official policy or position of any other agency, organization, employer, or company. The contents of this book are for informational and educational purposes only and are not intended to serve as professional advice, diagnosis, or treatment.

The information provided in this book is believed to be accurate and reliable as of the date of publication. However, it may include some errors or inaccuracies, and no warranty or guarantee is provided regarding the accuracy, timeliness, or applicability of the content.

Readers are encouraged to consult with professional philosophers, educators, or other qualified professionals where appropriate for personalized advice. The author(s) and publisher shall not be liable for any loss, damage, or harm caused or alleged to be caused, directly or indirectly, by the information or ideas contained, suggested, or referenced in this book.

By reading this book, the reader acknowledges and agrees that they are solely responsible for how they interpret and apply the information contained herein.

This book may also include references to other works, studies, and sources. These references are provided for further reading and exploration and do not imply endorsement or validation of the specific theories, viewpoints, or interpretations presented in those works.

Meet Your Inner Cast of Characters: The Id, Ego, and Superego

Ever wondered why you sometimes feel pulled in different directions? Why you crave that extra slice of cake even when you're full, or why you feel guilty for wanting it in the first place? Well, a famous psychologist named Sigmund Freud had some intriguing ideas about what's happening inside our minds.

Freud, often considered the father of psychoanalysis, believed that our minds are like a stage, with a cast of characters constantly interacting. He called these characters the Id, Ego, and Superego. Think of them as the impulsive child, the rational adult, and the moral judge, respectively.

The Id: Your Inner Child

The Id is the most primitive part of our personality. It's like a demanding child who wants what it wants, right now! It operates on the "pleasure principle," seeking immediate gratification of our basic needs and desires, like food, sex, and comfort. Ever had a sudden urge to do something impulsive, like splurge on a shopping spree or indulge in a risky behavior? That's your Id speaking.

The Superego: Your Inner Moral Compass

The Superego is like the strict parent or teacher who tells us what's right and wrong. It represents our internalized moral standards and values, often learned from our parents and society. The Superego strives for perfection and makes us feel guilty when we don't live up to its expectations. It's that nagging voice in your head that tells you to resist temptation and do the "right" thing.

The Ego: The Peacemaker

Caught in the middle of this inner tug-of-war is the Ego, the rational adult of the group. The Ego operates on the "reality principle," trying to find practical ways to satisfy the Id's desires while also considering the Superego's moral constraints. It's like a skilled negotiator, constantly balancing our impulses with our values and the demands of the real world.

A Dynamic System

Freud believed that our personality is a dynamic system, with these three forces constantly interacting and sometimes conflicting. A healthy balance is crucial. A dominant Id might lead to impulsive and reckless behavior, while a dominant Superego might result in excessive guilt and rigidity. The Ego's role is to find that sweet spot, where we can satisfy our needs and desires in a way that aligns with our values and the expectations of society.

Understanding this inner cast of characters can be incredibly insightful. It can help us make sense of our own behaviors, motivations, and conflicts. It can also shed light on our relationships with others, as we recognize that everyone has their own unique Id, Ego, and Superego dynamics at play.

So, the next time you feel conflicted or struggle with temptation, take a moment to consider which of your inner characters is taking the lead. Are you giving in to your impulsive Id, adhering to your strict Superego, or finding a balanced solution through your rational Ego? By understanding these forces within us, we can gain greater self-awareness and ultimately make more conscious choices in our lives.

Chapter 1

The Id - Your Wild Side

Think of the Id as the wild child inside of you, the one who wants what it wants, when it wants it. It's the part of your personality that's driven by pure pleasure and instinct. Imagine a toddler throwing a tantrum because they can't have the candy they want - that's your Id in action!

The Pleasure Principle:

The Id operates on what Freud called the "pleasure principle." It's like a little hedonist, constantly seeking pleasure and avoiding pain. It doesn't care about rules, consequences, or anyone else's feelings. It just wants to feel good, right now!

Primary Process Thinking:

The Id thinks in a very simple, illogical way. It doesn't understand reason, logic, or delayed gratification. It's all about immediate satisfaction. It's like a hungry baby crying for food - it doesn't care how the food gets there, it just wants to eat!

Instinctual Drives: Eros and Thanatos

Freud believed that the Id is driven by two basic instincts: Eros, the life instinct, and Thanatos, the death instinct. Eros is responsible for our desires for love, sex, and connection. It's the force that drives us to create, reproduce, and seek pleasure. Thanatos, on the other hand, is associated with aggression, destruction, and self-destruction. It's the darker side of our nature, the part that can lead to risky behaviors, anger, and even violence.

The Id in Everyday Life

Your Id is at play whenever you feel a sudden urge to do something impulsive. It's the voice that tells you to eat the whole pizza, buy the expensive shoes, or skip work to go to the beach. It's also the force behind our more primal emotions, like anger, lust, and envy.

Why Understand Your Id?

While the Id may seem like the "bad guy" of our personality, it's actually an essential part of who we are. It's the source of our energy, creativity, and passion. Without it, we would lack motivation and drive. However, it's important to recognize and understand our Id so that we can manage its impulses and channel its energy in healthy ways.

Ignoring your Id can lead to repressed desires and frustrations, which can manifest in unhealthy ways, like overeating, addiction, or impulsive behavior. On the other hand, giving in to your Id all the time can lead to reckless and self-destructive behavior. The key is to find a balance. By understanding your Id, you can learn to recognize its influence and make conscious choices that align with your values and goals. You can harness its energy for creative pursuits, healthy relationships, and a fulfilling life.

Chapter 2

The Superego – Your Inner Jiminy Cricket

If the Id is the wild child, then the Superego is the wise and sometimes overly cautious cricket perched on your shoulder, constantly whispering in your ear about right and wrong. It's the moral compass of your personality, striving for perfection and upholding the values you've learned from your family, culture, and society.

The Morality Principle:

Unlike the pleasure-seeking Id, the Superego operates on the "morality principle." It's concerned with upholding ethical standards and ideals, even if it means sacrificing immediate gratification. It's the voice that urges you to be honest, kind, and responsible.

Conscience and Ego Ideal:

The Superego has two main components: the conscience and the ego ideal. The conscience is like your inner critic, punishing you with guilt and shame when you break the rules. It's that nagging feeling you get when you do something you know is wrong. The ego ideal, on the other hand, is your vision of the perfect self, the person you strive to become. It's the image of the kind, generous, successful individual you aspire to be.

Internalized Values:

Your Superego is shaped by the values and beliefs you've internalized from your parents, teachers, religious figures, and society as a whole. It reflects the cultural norms and expectations you've been exposed to throughout your life. For example, if you were raised in a strict household with strong moral values, your Superego might be more rigid and demanding.

The Superego in Everyday Life:

Your Superego is at work whenever you feel a sense of guilt, shame, or pride. It's the voice that tells you to return the extra change you received, to help someone in need, or to study instead of going out with friends. It's also the force that drives you to achieve your goals and live up to your own expectations.

The Superego and Guilt:

The Superego plays a crucial role in shaping our behavior, but it can also be a source of great anxiety and guilt. When we fail to live up to our own moral standards or the expectations of others, the Superego punishes us with feelings of guilt and shame. While a healthy dose of guilt can motivate us to do better, an overly harsh Superego can lead to excessive self-criticism and even depression.

Finding a Balance:

Just like the Id, the Superego is an essential part of our personality. It helps us navigate the complexities of social life, make ethical decisions, and strive for personal growth. However, it's important to find a balance between the demands of the Superego and the desires of the Id. A healthy Superego provides guidance and support, while an overly strict one can stifle our creativity, joy, and spontaneity.

By understanding your Superego, you can learn to discern between genuine moral guidance and excessive self-criticism. You can develop a more compassionate and realistic view of yourself, accepting your imperfections while still striving to be the best version of yourself.

Chapter 3

The Ego – The Master Negotiator

Imagine your mind as a bustling city with competing factions. The Id is the chaotic crowd, demanding immediate satisfaction, while the Superego is the strict police force, enforcing rules and order. In the midst of this chaos, the Ego emerges as the savvy diplomat, the master negotiator who strives to maintain peace and harmony.

The Reality Principle:

Unlike the Id's pleasure-seeking and the Superego's moralizing, the Ego operates on the "reality principle." It's the pragmatic problem-solver, the voice of reason that takes into account the constraints of the real world. The Ego understands that we can't always get what we want, and that sometimes we need to delay gratification or find compromises.

Secondary Process Thinking:

The Ego uses a more sophisticated and logical way of thinking than the Id. It employs "secondary process thinking," which involves planning, reasoning, and problem-solving. It assesses situations, considers consequences, and weighs different options before making decisions. It's the part of you that makes a to-do list, budgets your money, or comes up with a creative solution to a challenge.

Balancing Act:

The Ego's primary role is to mediate between the Id and the Superego. It's like a skilled tightrope walker, carefully balancing the demands of our primal urges with our moral values. It strives to find solutions that satisfy both the Id's desire for pleasure and the Superego's need for approval.

The Ego in Everyday Life:

Your Ego is at play whenever you make a decision, big or small. It's the part of you that resists the urge to buy that expensive item you can't afford, the voice that tells you to study for an exam instead of binge-watching your favorite show, and the force that pushes you to apologize when you've hurt someone's feelings.

The Importance of a Strong Ego:

A strong and healthy Ego is essential for navigating the complexities of life. It allows us to adapt to our environment, make sound decisions, and build fulfilling relationships. A weak Ego, on the other hand, can leave us vulnerable to anxiety, depression, and other mental health issues.

When the Ego is overwhelmed by the demands of the Id or the Superego, it can resort to defense mechanisms like denial, repression, or projection. While these mechanisms can provide temporary relief, they can also lead to long-term problems if they become habitual.

Nurturing Your Ego:

Building a strong Ego involves developing self-awareness, emotional intelligence, and coping skills. It means learning to recognize and manage our emotions, set healthy boundaries, and communicate effectively. It also involves practicing self-care and seeking support when needed.

By strengthening your Ego, you empower yourself to make conscious choices, take responsibility for your actions, and create a life that is both fulfilling and aligned with your values.

Chapter 4

Inner Turmoil: When Your Mind Plays Defense

Imagine a boxing ring inside your head, with the **Id** and **Superego** as fierce opponents. The Id throws punches of desire and impulse, while the Superego counters with jabs of guilt and judgment. Caught in the middle, the **Ego** struggles to referee this inner brawl. Sometimes, the Ego manages to keep the peace, but other times, the conflict escalates, leading to inner turmoil and anxiety.

The Ego, ever resourceful, has a few tricks up its sleeve to handle these conflicts. Freud called them "**defense mechanisms.**" These are unconscious strategies that the Ego uses to protect itself from overwhelming emotions and maintain a sense of balance. Let's explore some of the most common ones:

Repression: The Memory Eraser

Repression is like pushing unwanted thoughts, feelings, or memories into the basement of your mind, hoping they'll stay hidden forever. It's the Ego's way of saying, "I can't deal with this right now, so I'm going to pretend it doesn't exist." While repression can provide temporary relief, it can also lead to unresolved issues that resurface later in life.

Denial: The Reality Distorter

Denial is the refusal to accept a painful reality. It's like wearing blinders to block out something you don't want to see. A person might deny a serious illness, a loved one's death, or their own addiction. Denial can be a coping mechanism in the short term, but it can also prevent someone from seeking help and addressing the underlying problem.

Projection: The Blame Shifter

Projection involves attributing your own unacceptable thoughts, feelings, or impulses to someone else. For example, if you're angry at your partner but feel guilty about it, you might accuse them of being angry at you. Projection can be a way to avoid taking responsibility for your own emotions, but it can also damage relationships.

Displacement: The Redirected Anger

Displacement is when you redirect your anger or frustration from its original source to a safer target. For example, if you're angry at your boss but can't express it directly, you might come home and yell at your family. While displacement can provide temporary relief, it can also create conflict and harm innocent people.

Sublimation: The Creative Outlet

Sublimation is considered one of the healthiest defense mechanisms. It involves channeling unacceptable impulses into socially acceptable activities. For example, a person with aggressive tendencies might become a boxer, or someone with a strong sexual drive might become an artist. Sublimation allows us to express our emotions in a constructive way, without harming ourselves or others.

Healthy vs. Unhealthy Use of Defense Mechanisms:

While defense mechanisms can be useful in managing difficult emotions, they can also become problematic if they are overused or used to avoid dealing with underlying issues. A **healthy Ego** is able to use defense mechanisms in moderation, while also facing and processing difficult emotions. An **unhealthy Ego**, on the other hand, may rely on defense mechanisms excessively, leading to denial, distortion of reality, and impaired relationships.

By understanding the different defense mechanisms and their potential impact, we can gain insight into our own behavior and the behavior of others. We can learn to recognize when we are using defense mechanisms to avoid facing reality and develop healthier ways of coping with difficult emotions.

Chapter 5

Your Inner Cast on the Big Screen: Id, Ego, and Superego in Pop Culture

Freud's concepts of the Id, Ego, and Superego may seem like abstract psychological theories, but they've actually had a profound impact on popular culture. These ideas have been woven into the fabric of countless stories, songs, and films, often in ways that are both entertaining and insightful. By exploring these representations, we can deepen our understanding of these concepts and see how they resonate with our own experiences.

Literature:

Robert Louis Stevenson's classic novella "Strange Case of Dr. Jekyll and Mr. Hyde" is a prime example of the Id and Superego in conflict. Dr. Jekyll, the respectable physician, represents the Ego, struggling to control the impulsive and destructive urges of his alter ego, Mr. Hyde, who embodies the unbridled Id. The story serves as a cautionary tale about the dangers of repressing our darker impulses and the importance of maintaining a balance between our opposing desires.

Film:

In the cult classic "Fight Club," the unnamed narrator embodies the Ego, trapped in a mundane existence and yearning for something more. His alter ego, Tyler Durden, represents the rebellious and charismatic Id, encouraging him to break free from societal constraints and embrace chaos. The film explores the tension between conformity and rebellion, and the dangers of allowing the Id to run unchecked.

Television:

"The Simpsons" offers a humorous take on Freudian theory. Homer Simpson, with his insatiable appetite for donuts and beer, is the quintessential Id character. His wife Marge, with her unwavering moral compass, represents the Superego. Bart, the mischievous prankster, embodies the Id's rebellious spirit, while Lisa, the intelligent and conscientious daughter, personifies the Ego's rational voice. The show's comedic exploration of these characters allows us to laugh at our own inner conflicts and recognize the universal nature of these struggles.

Music:

The Backseat Lovers' song "Super Ego" delves into the complexities of the Superego, exploring themes of guilt, shame, and the pressure to conform to societal expectations. The lyrics capture the internal dialogue between the Ego and the Superego, as the singer grapples with conflicting desires and the fear of judgment. The song serves as a reminder that we are all subject to these internal struggles and that it's important to find a balance between our own needs and the expectations of others.

Relevance in Contemporary Society:

The enduring popularity of these stories and others like them suggests that Freud's concepts continue to resonate with us on a deep level. We all experience the inner conflict between our desires, values, and the demands of the real world. By recognizing these forces within ourselves, we can gain greater self-awareness and make more conscious choices in our lives.

Popular culture provides a valuable mirror for reflecting on our own psychological makeup. By identifying with characters and their struggles, we can gain a deeper understanding of our own motivations, conflicts, and defense mechanisms. This awareness can empower us to make positive changes, cultivate healthier relationships, and ultimately live more fulfilling lives.

In conclusion, the Id, Ego, and Superego are not just theoretical constructs; they are living, breathing entities within each of us. By exploring their manifestations in popular culture, we can gain a deeper appreciation for their complexity and relevance in our own lives. Whether it's through the pages of a novel, the scenes of a film, or the lyrics of a song, these stories can help us navigate our inner landscapes and find a harmonious balance between our conflicting desires.

Chapter 6

The Power of Insight: Applying Freudian Theory to Your Life

Understanding the interplay of the Id, Ego, and Superego isn't just an intellectual exercise; it's a powerful tool for personal growth, healthier relationships, and improved mental well-being. Let's explore how this knowledge can be applied in various areas of your life:

Self-Understanding and Personal Growth:

- **Identifying Your Inner Drivers:** By recognizing the different forces at play within your mind, you can gain a deeper understanding of your motivations, desires, and behaviors. This awareness can help you make more conscious choices and break free from patterns that no longer serve you.
- **Managing Your Impulses:** Understanding the Id's influence can help you manage impulsive behaviors and develop strategies for delaying gratification. This can lead to better decision-making and greater self-control.

- **Cultivating Self-Compassion:** Recognizing the role of the Superego in self-criticism can help you develop a more compassionate and accepting attitude towards yourself. This can reduce feelings of guilt and shame and promote self-love.
- **Strengthening Your Ego:** By learning to identify and manage the demands of the Id and Superego, you can strengthen your Ego's ability to find balanced solutions. This can lead to greater resilience, improved problem-solving skills, and a more fulfilling life.

Relationships and Interpersonal Dynamics:

- **Understanding Others' Behavior:** By recognizing the influence of the Id, Ego, and Superego in others, you can gain a deeper understanding of their motivations and behaviors. This can lead to greater empathy, improved communication, and stronger relationships.
- **Resolving Conflicts:** Understanding the dynamics of the Id, Ego, and Superego can help you navigate conflicts more effectively. By recognizing the underlying needs and fears driving each party, you can find win-win solutions and strengthen your relationships.
- **Setting Healthy Boundaries:** Understanding the importance of a strong Ego can help you set healthy boundaries in your relationships. This means knowing when to say no, when to compromise, and when to prioritize your own needs.

Mental Health and Therapy:

- **Psychoanalysis and Psychotherapy:** Freud's theories form the basis of psychoanalysis, a form of therapy that explores the unconscious mind and helps individuals understand and resolve internal conflicts. By exploring their Id, Ego, and Superego dynamics, people can gain insight into the root causes of their emotional and behavioral issues and develop healthier coping mechanisms.
- **Managing Anxiety and Depression:** Understanding the role of the Superego in self-criticism and guilt can help individuals manage anxiety and depression. By developing a more compassionate inner voice and challenging negative self-talk, people can improve their mental well-being.
- **Treating Addiction and Compulsive Behaviors:** Understanding the Id's role in impulsive behaviors can be helpful in treating addiction and other compulsive disorders. By learning to manage their impulses and find healthier ways to satisfy their needs, individuals can overcome these challenges.

Incorporating Freudian concepts into your daily life can be a transformative experience. By understanding the forces at play within your mind, you can gain greater self-awareness, build stronger relationships, and improve your overall well-being. Whether you're seeking personal growth, navigating interpersonal challenges, or addressing mental health concerns, Freudian theory offers valuable insights and tools for living a more fulfilling life.

Chapter 7

Your Inner Symphony

As we've journeyed through the realms of the Id, Ego, and Superego, it's clear that Freud's structural model offers a captivating lens through which to view our inner lives. We've seen how these three forces, like instruments in an orchestra, each play a distinct role in shaping our thoughts, feelings, and actions.

The Id, our impulsive and pleasure-seeking conductor, provides the raw energy and passion that fuels our desires. The Superego, our moral compass and inner critic, sets the ethical boundaries and strives for perfection. And the Ego, our rational mediator, navigates the complex terrain between these two opposing forces, seeking a harmonious balance.

While Freud's theories may have been developed over a century ago, they continue to resonate with us today. The struggles between our desires, values, and the demands of reality are timeless human experiences. By understanding these dynamics, we gain a deeper appreciation for the complexity of our inner world and the forces that shape our behavior.

As you continue on your journey of self-discovery, remember that your inner landscape is a dynamic and ever-evolving ecosystem. The Id, Ego, and Superego are not static entities, but rather fluid forces that interact in a constant dance. By becoming aware of their influence, you can begin to choreograph this dance with greater intention and grace.

Embrace your Id's playful spirit, harness its energy for creative expression, and find healthy outlets for your passions. Listen to your Superego's moral guidance, but don't let it become a harsh critic that stifles your joy and spontaneity. And most importantly, nurture your Ego, the wise mediator that can help you find balance and fulfillment in all areas of your life.

By exploring your inner landscape with curiosity and compassion, you can unlock the hidden potential within you and live a life that is both authentic and meaningful. Remember, the journey of self-discovery is a lifelong adventure, and the rewards are immeasurable. So, embrace your inner symphony, and let its melodies guide you toward a richer, more fulfilling existence.

About Freudian Trips

Welcome to Freudian Trips, your dedicated platform for diving deep into the world of psychology. We are more than just a YouTube channel or a book publisher. We are a beacon of enlightenment, making complex psychological concepts accessible and engaging for all.

Our YouTube channel is a rich repository of psychology made simple. We take the profound and often complex ideas from the world of psychology and break them down into digestible, easy-to-understand content. From the foundational theories of Freud to the cognitive insights of Piaget, we cover a broad spectrum of psychological schools and thoughts, making psychology accessible to everyone, regardless of their background or prior knowledge.

As a book publisher, we take the same approach, transforming intricate psychological theories into comprehensible narratives. Our books are not just collections of words, but vessels of wisdom that make psychology approachable and relatable. We believe that psychology should not be confined to academic circles, but should be available to all who seek to understand the human mind and behavior.

At Freudian Trips, we believe in the power of curiosity and the pursuit of knowledge. We are here to stoke the fires of your curiosity, to guide you on your intellectual journey, and to help you navigate the fascinating world of psychology.

If you are someone who is not afraid to question, to explore, and to learn, then you are in the right place. Join us on this journey of exploration, as we make psychology easy to understand, one concept at a time.

Be sure to visit our Youtube channel at:
www.freudiantrips.com/youtube

You can also visit us on the web at www.freudiantrips.com

Welcome to The Freudian Trip community. Stay curious. Stay enlightened.